Love Is NOT Enough!

ISBN: 978-1-7349160-9-6

Library of Congress Cataloging-in-Publication Data

Scripture quotations: Taken from the Holy Bible: New Living Translation (NLT).
Wheaton, Ill: Tyndale House Publishers, 2004 and The King James Version.
Dallas, Brown Books Publishing, 2004.

Professional Editing: SynergyEd Consulting/ synergyedconsulting.com

Photography: Williams Photography, J. Alexander Online -
www.jalexanderonline.com

Graphics: Greenlight Creations Graphics Designs

Cover Design: Greenlight Creations - glightcreations.com/
glightcreations@gmail.com

Publishing & Marketing: SHERO Publishing.com

getpublished@sheropublishing.com
S H E R O P U B L I S H I N G . C O M

OLAUNDA GREEN
LIFE COACH / RELATIONSHIP STRATEGIST

O L A U N D A G R E E N . C O M

3

TABLE OF CONTENTS

Dedication

     I dedicate this book to the love of my life, my best friend and confidant, Bruce Green. Thank you for believing in this project, pushing me when I wanted to give up and allowing me to share our story! I could not have done this without your support. Our openness is going to help those headed toward marriage, avoid many of the pitfalls we have faced. This book will also help those already married, HEAL, knowing that if we can overcome, so can they! Our tests have produced a testimony. Our experiences have made us who we are today and for that I am grateful. There is no other person I want to share this journey of marriage with. I love you Bae!

Olaunda

Preface

Several years ago, I attended my daughter's field day at her elementary school. Parents were asked to volunteer time to oversee game stations situated in various places throughout the playground for grades K through 5. Since my daughter was a kindergartener at that time, I naturally volunteered for grades K-2.

I arrived at the school on a hot, 95-degree day to find all sorts of stations to fit each child's desire, from the water balloon toss to the relay race. At first, I wasn't pressed about which station I would be assigned; at that moment, my only concern was staying cool. However, as I proceeded further down a hill toward the field, I saw a thick, brown rope laying across the mud-soaked ground, which I intuitively knew was meant for the tug-of-war game. It had rained very hard the day before and despite the rise in temperature, the ground was still saturated with water. Quickly my openness to volunteer for ANY game station suddenly turned to stark regret. Yet, I couldn't turn back and head for my car because I had committed my time. Most importantly, I knew my daughter, Simone, expected to see me there.

While I didn't care about getting hit by water balloons, I did care about getting dirty. I remembered from my own play days that tug-of-war was a messy, unpredictable, dirty game. So, I knew if I were assigned to the tug-of-war station, I would get splashed with mud as I would have to stand there in the middle of the sparring teams to referee the game. I couldn't help imagining the students pulling with all their might, while sliding forcefully through the mud as though they were coming in for a homerun during a baseball game. I began to think about how dirty the kids would be and the fact that I would probably be cleaning off mud all day; the mud in which the children would purposely try to fall and splash. I mean, what kid doesn't like to play in mud?

Anyone close to me knows that I don't like to be hot and definitely not DIRTY. I mean, no way was I getting dirty!

After some debate in my head, I went over to the volunteer sign-up table and stated my request—for anything but the tug-of-war. I asked the parent captain if assignments had been made or if we could choose. She stated that since I was early, I had first choice on the game station I wanted to manage. Crisis averted! I quickly put my name beside the hula hoop station and got myself over there before anyone else got any ideas.

Although humorous in nature, this depiction of my daughter's field day is exactly how we are at times, in relationships with our significant others. That is, we want to stay cool and comfortable and do what suits our taste. We only want to roll with what feels familiar: those things to which we have been accustomed. No one wants to deal with the dirtiness of "tug-of-war" in relationships. No one wants to be dragged through the mud of unpredictability, misunderstanding or any deviation from the expected. Sometimes our partner crosses the line and finds himself or herself in the middle of the mud pit because maybe you jerked the rope suddenly or tugged too hard. In other words, perhaps you yanked the rope just when they were pulling on their end to get a point across; or maybe you purposely stepped back, let go of the rope, causing them to fall face-first into the mud.

Fortunately, there is a way to balance the "tug-of-war" that goes on in relationships by first knowing this fact: LOVE alone IS NOT enough to sustain a successful relationship and more importantly, a great marriage! Rather, great relationships are sustained and heavily influenced by many things. There is no balancing act in relationships without multiple elements and all must play an equal starring role. Falling in love without recognizing this will land you in the mud. You see, relationships involve a "tug-of-war" where partners find themselves giving a little and sometimes taking a lot. If you are dating and you want to be married, there are some important things you need to know first! It's awesome being in love but for any relationship to thrive, you've got to know, **Love Is Not Enough**!

CHAPTER ONE

My Reason Why

So, I'm sure you might be wondering why I'm writing this book or what even qualifies me to give any type of marriage advice. You may also question my motivation or my inspiration as a pre-marriage coach. Well, here goes. Bruce and I have now been married for 15 years and I would say we are in the best place we have ever been: living our best life. However, take note, it hasn't always been this way! In 2008, just three years into our marriage, my husband and I survived a very difficult storm. This storm involved so many different layers: ranging from infidelity to legal turmoil, which nearly landed my husband in prison. He ended up losing his career as a police officer. Then less than 8 months later I found out my job was being phased out. We went from living the American dream, well at least from the outside looking in, straight to bankruptcy court. We couldn't communicate effectively, we were at each other's throat and our relationship felt more like roommates than marriage. This period of my life between 2008-2009 was an absolute nightmare and is still a blur today. However, with counseling, much work and lots of prayer, we made it by the help and favor of God! Consequently, I went back to school and received my masters in counseling with a concentration in life coaching. Today, I provide pre-marriage coaching to dating, engaged, and newly- married couples. Coaching couples often feels more like refereeing, hence my outfit on the front book cover! Helping couples succeed in marriage has become my passion. Pre-marriage coaching helps couples define roles, expectations, and

9

explore various ideals brought into the relationship from a partner's past that need to be addressed. Well, enough about that. We will dive more deeply into coaching later on.

When We First Met

I still remember the first time I met Bruce. It was August 2003. Our first few hours together was spent at a Sunday evening "singing" program at a church back home in Dunn, North Carolina. Shortly before the service, we were introduced by mutual family friends. Our crew sat together, beside one another on the same pew. I was secretly checking Bruce out on the sly! I watched him throughout the service taking note of how he clapped his hands and tapped his feet to the music. He was very handsome, nice, seemed respectable and smelled so good! About midway through the program I leaned over to tell my sister that I was getting ready to head out. I then told Bruce it was nice to meet him and he asked if he could walk me out to my car, and I said "yes." We tipped out of the service as not to disturb anyone. As we were walking to the parking lot, I thought to myself, this is nice and I smiled on the inside. It felt good to have someone care.

We talked for a few minutes at my car and then as I proceeded to open the door, he popped the question! "Do you mind if I get your number?" In my head, I knew where this was going, but did I really? You see, while his exterior was nice, I was not ready to take a chance on his interior. I had had enough games played and was trying to get out of another relationship that was dead and going nowhere real fast! So, I reluctantly said, "NO." I told him I didn't think that was a good idea as I was just getting out of another relationship. Then he asked if he could give me his number in case I changed my mind. I agreed. So he took out a pen and jotted his number down for me on a piece of paper. I said, "goodbye" and I drove away. As soon as I was out of his eyesight, I rolled down the window and tossed the slip of paper with his number out and watched if float away on the night air. I know, I know, how cold of me right?? Over the years, we have told this story a million times and laughed. However, when the event happened, I was so broken and confused that I could not fathom how to start over or begin to move on. I wasn't ready to take a chance on a new relationship.

Several weeks went by which turned into months. Then on the night of New Year's Eve, I saw Bruce, back home, at yet another church program. We had this big celebration at the local community center where several churches came together to ring in the New Year. Many people came from all over and the center was packed. When the service was over, I saw Bruce outside. Initially I didn't feel anything, but when I saw him walk around to the passenger door of his car to open it for another young lady I was dumb-founded. He wasn't paying any attention to me. The guy who seemed so persistent months ago to get to know me, had moved on. In that moment, seeing him and the young lady together, made me feel some type of way. Was it jealousy? No!! No way could I be jealous when I had my chance. However, the logic in my head, was no match for what I felt in my heart. The feelings I felt that night were very real. For the first time, I knew I really liked him.

Several more months went by and I was having a conversation with his cousin; he was the one who had introduced us. I asked how Bruce was doing and if he was still in a relationship. His cousin went on to say that Bruce was doing great, was not in a relationship anymore and had actually asked about me not long ago. That same day I told him to give Bruce my phone number the next time he asked about me. Well, unbeknownst to me, they talked later that evening and Bruce called me the same night. We talked on the phone for hours as if we had known each other all our lives. I told my sister the next day that I thought Bruce could be my husband. It wasn't a certainty, but a sense of comfort I felt when we talked, a certain reminder of home, as if with him was where I should be. We didn't know it at the time; but, we had gone to rival high schools in different cities but within the same county. Yet, it wasn't until after college that we were introduced. It's a small world and amazing how God can bring things full circle in his timing.

After that night, our telephone conversations were frequent. Bruce was still living back home in Dunn, but regularly came to visit me in Durham. Although I was giddy on the inside, I kept a hard exterior. I wouldn't let him kiss me or get too close. I felt more comfortable hanging out in groups than just me and him alone. I'm not sure what my problem was, but I think I was afraid to try and fully let go of my old relationship. I was dating Bruce but still keeping my options open just in case he turned out to be crazy and I needed to jump back. Then finally one day Bruce said, he was tired of playing games. Either I wanted to be with him or I didn't because he wanted a wife and was dating for marriage. So, I had to make a decision. Do I stay with what's familiar although it was killing me inside because it wasn't going anywhere, or do I step out and take a chance on something brand new? I still remember that day so vividly: the day I finally made up my mind and decided to be exclusive. I told Bruce I would be his girlfriend and from that point on our relationship took off.

We dated strong for an entire year and on July 30, 2004 he proposed. Eight months later, we were married. I remember having just one pre-marriage counseling session from our former pastor. Yes, I said just one!! We met in his office one Sunday after church and spent about an hour or so discussing major topic areas in marriage such as money, communication, and sex. I am ashamed to say it, but I don't think I pushed for more because I just believed that Bruce and I were destined to be together. I mean Bruce's pastor had prophesied to us that I was Bruce's appointed wife. So in my head I thought that relinquished me from the work. If God wanted us to be together then it was going to be okay. Right?? Ummm, no! Faith without works is dead. Just because God predestines or ordains a thing, does not release you from the work to make it great!

As blissful as things were at times, I did see some issues and personality flaws in the both of us early on, especially in how we handled conflict. However, I think Bruce and I chose to ignore them because we wanted to be married so badly. Besides, the proposal had already taken place and the ring was on my finger. This is why I tell couples to seek pre-marriage coaching in the dating process, at the moment they feel marriage potential. Pre-marriage counseling or coaching is essential and should be sought long before the proposal, the acceptance of a ring or setting a wedding date.

If people were honest, most couples only seek pre-marriage counseling or coaching to fulfill a prerequisite set by the pastor or minister performing their wedding ceremony. However, you must take the initiative early on, to learn more about your mate before feelings and emotions grow too deeply. Deep feelings can override the courage you may need to wait or in some instances, break up. During the sessions, you may realize that your partner is just not a good fit. Doing it the opposite way will cause you to push into something that would have been much easier to dissolve had you committed to doing the work up front.

Bruce and I got married in our mid-twenties in March of 2005. Looking back, we both acknowledge now that we were not ready to be married; as we were both still very immature. However, we fell into the social pressure to tie the knot because so many other couples around us were doing so. We enjoyed dating and hanging out with them and looked forward to being a part of the newly married crew. Subconsciously, I thought, it would all be so much fun. Little did I know, marriage is not all sunshine without any rain. Honestly, I actually don't know what I thought marriage would be. Maybe I thought it would be modeled after what I saw on television as many relationships on sitcoms and in movies are highly fantasized. The couples on television gaze into each others' eyes, as if everyday is Sunday; seemingly with no problems. The issue with this is, it's just not real. It is staged and rehearsed for perfection. So patterning yourself or your expectations after something that doesn't even exist will land you in a world of trouble.

The Real Issues

I was extremely head-strong and independent when we married. I had graduated from North Carolina Central University, (EAGLE PRIDE!!) at the top of my class! When I met my husband, I had my own money, my own car, my own apartment and a professional job. Unbeknownst to me, this left my husband little room to feel like the man and provide support to our marriage. I was so independent and thought I had everything worked out. While I was strong in those areas, I was very insecure and extremely skeptical going into our relationship because of some of the past hurts I had experienced - we will get to those in the next chapter. So, I started our relationship with lots of baggage and my husband paid for many things that had nothing to do with him. I accused him of things that he wasn't even doing because the situation seemed familiar, yet not the same. I had not truly healed and become whole as a woman. I was so dependent on Bruce to affirm me, which on the surface is fine. However, when you are so reliant on another person's affirmation that you fall apart the minute you don't get it, that is dangerous. You cannot make anyone else responsible for your own happiness. Hear me loud and clear, that is your job! Only you can make yourself happy. Happiness and joy comes from within and expecting your significant other to be responsible for your happiness is unfair.

13

I am the extrovert in the relationship and Bruce is the introvert. However, while quiet, he can still be extremely stubborn at times. Advising him or telling him what to do back then was out of the question. This stance left me little room to be his wife and help-mate. We didn't know how to temper our dominant sides. We continued to argue and disagree so much that things began to compile and distance set in between us, which allowed for outside influences into our marriage. The distance that grew between us, made us both look for solace in other people. By our third year of marriage, we had both cheated on each other. Had we worked to leverage our unique personalities early on and figured out how to communicate effectively, we would have probably avoided a lot of heartache that we experienced. We had not clearly defined roles and expectations which should have been done in pre-marriage counseling. Having the right tools in your relationship tool box is key to combating issues and resolving them before they become substantial. We will discuss more on effective communication and compromise in the following chapters.

CHAPTER ONE NOTES

_____

_____

_____

_____

_____

_____

_____

_____

_____

_____

_____

_____

_____

_____

_____

_____

_____

_____

_____

_____

_____

CHAPTER ONE:

Reflection & Application

1. Are you ready to embark on the journey of dating?
   How do you know?

   _____

   _____

   _____

   _____

   _____

   _____

   _____

2. Explain why pre-marriage coaching is important. Will you seek
   pre-marriage coaching in your dating relationship, before marriage,
   as the author suggested?

   _____

   _____

   _____

   _____

   _____

   _____

   _____

CHAPTER TWO

Why Are You Dating??

*G*rowing up, my parents had a rule that we had to be at least sixteen years old to date. While totally reasonable in theory, this was difficult for me once I became smitten by a young trumpet player in our high school's marching band, during my freshman year. At that point in time, I was only fifteen years old, so the thought of waiting another year to date seemed like an eternity. I really liked the guy, and I wanted to find a way to get to know him better without disobeying my parents' rule. Unlike today, there were no cell phones, so the only option to talk was using a landline phone. The county where my high school was located was very rural and believe it or not, calling from one part to the other in many instances was considered long distance. Unfortunately for us, this was our situation; therefore, talking for hours on end was not happening.

I had enjoyed playing clarinet in the band since middle school and wanted to try something different. Like I stated earlier, my friend played the trumpet and was more than willing to help me explore learning to play a brass instrument. My dad allowed him to come over to our home a couple nights a week to coach me with learning to play the new instrument. I remember my dad instructing us to go into the living room to practice but to leave the door open. I didn't have any issues with this because I just wanted to learn the trumpet and spend more time with this guy. In my mind this was the best of both worlds. After a few lessons, my dad realized that these trumpet lessons were a little more than "trumpet lessons". I was crushing on this guy and trying to find a loophole around the dating rule in our home. While my infatuation was innocent in nature, my desire to be around him clouded my better judgment and nearly got me grounded! At that time, I had no objective for dating, I just knew I liked him a lot because we enjoyed similar things and we got along great.

The Dating Game

We all long to experience some of these same qualities even in adult relationships. However, if not careful, you will find yourself behaving like a giddy, starry-eyed fifteen-year-old teenager with no dating wisdom. Adult dating has much less room for exploration if you want it to end in marriage. So, you can't get caught up in your feelings too soon. On the contrary, you must think logistically and practically. The reason many singles fail in the dating game is because they have no objectives for dating. They can't even articulate clearly why they want to date. Some of their reasons for dating range from wanting to "have a good time" to "finding a mate". Whatever your preference, you must be clear from the start in your intentions to accomplish the desired end. It is important to know that dating is still not a universal practice. In many cultures, the idea of a man and woman arranging a series of times to get together, for whatever purpose, would be considered taboo. Yet many of these cultures have a long history of stable marriages which shows that there is more to a successful marriage than simply dating or even love.

I don't believe anyone gets married with the intention to get divorced. Most people who are divorced today report having been in love and feeling cared for at the time of marriage, so what happened? Why do things go south? The answer is heavily predicated on the fact that most people misunderstand the nature of love in relationships. While love is a needed element, it is not everything. People think that if they are in love, then that's enough; but love is not enough. Romantic love is very popular in Western culture because it is bred from the idea that love happens to us and it is something very magical. While love may be experienced in this way in the beginning of a relationship it is not sustainable without other needed ingredients.

20

You must determine your purpose in dating, as people date for various reasons. So, go ahead, ask yourself, why am I dating, or why do I want to date? In order to make sense out of anything you do, you must know why you are doing it. The same is true for dating. I would imagine that most people are dating to find that special someone to have children with, evolve into a better version of themselves, and to discover with whom to spend the rest of their lives. However, has it ever occurred to you that there is a subset of the population that's just not the marrying type? Consequently, what will be your disposition if you fall for someone who does not desire marriage, yet you do? Will you stay in the relationship with the intention to convince them otherwise, or will you be brave enough to move on? These are the kinds of questions in which you need answers before falling madly in love with someone. Relationships are forever changing as we all experience evolutions in life, but few stop to analyze why some relationships work and some do not. I believe it has much to do with the individual intentions of the couple from the beginning. If one person is dating to have fun and the other desires marriage, then the relationship won't work. Both individuals must share the same objectives for dating and move succinctly towards that purpose. To help singles navigate the dating scene and prepare for marriage, I developed a strategy called Date SMART (Sharing My Affection in Real Time).

Date SMART- Sharing My Affection in Real Time

SHARING

Learning to share is one of the first life lessons taught to young children. Whether we are teaching them to share a toy, give a hug or allow another child to have some of their snack, it's still some level of sharing. If only relationship sharing was that simple. Sharing involves your ability to do without; to put someone else's desire above your own. In a relationship it can't be mine, mine, mine! While this chant is accepted in toddlerhood, there is no place for it in achieving meaningful long-lasting relationships in adulthood and definitely not in marriage. As you think about dating to marry, you must expand your mindset from one to two; from me to us.

As a single person your only concern is you. There is no one else to consider when deciding what to have for dinner, how late to hang out with

21

friends or even where to plant roots to live. However, when you join your life to someone else, there is an immense amount of sharing that spans from emotional to tangible. Two different lives become one and every element of those lives must be put in proper perspective to be successful.

One of the reasons why my husband and I decided to buy a house after we got married and forgo our individual apartments was to avoid, what I like to call the "MINE" syndrome. This is when you remind your significant other in heated arguments that something is yours. This is easy to do when your partner irritates you or is not going along with something that you want to do. That is why you must create a level playing field as much as possible so you both feel that things equally belong to you both. I knew we didn't need to stay in my apartment, that was in MY name and that I used MY credit to obtain because it would be too easy to throw that into his face or vice versa.

MY AFFECTION

Another aspect of "Dating SMART" is learning to control affection. So let's say you go on your first date and the other person says that it is their desire to be married and they are looking to find that special someone. So, now what? While you will be excited to hear this, don't lose it. Proceed slowly with caution. My former pastor used to tell the singles that they needed to date people through each of the four seasons of the year- fall, winter, spring and summer. While most of us laughed, there really was some significance to this suggestion when you think about it. The reason is because people can be moody and change like the weather. There are people who become depressed in winter, so can you imagine your surprise meeting them in summer and going through fall with them and then BOOM, you don't even recognize them come November! The point is, be patient. Don't put anything past anyone until you really get to know them. Date them for understanding. Date to really get to know those little annoying habits and things that you would rather they not do. Once these things are identified, then they can be addressed. However, if your aim is just to be married no matter what, you will end up having to deal with quite a bit for which you did not bargain.

So with this in mind, once you meet someone and the conversation strikes up- because something has obviously attracted you to the person, you need to think smart and not allow your emotions to override good judgment.

22

You want to be friendly and open but not desperate. Desperation is a major turn off but confidence is attractive. Even if you have no other options, you need to act like others are beating your door down trying to get to know you. The initial conversation might just be a playful flirtation, or it could lead to an invitation to go out for a date. If this is the case, no matter how excited you might feel, you need to keep things in perspective and think of how you are going to find out the person's intentions. This question needs to be asked on the first date. Yes, I said it, "THE FIRST DATE". You don't have time to waste on people who don't know where they are going. Don't ask if they want to be married, but rather what's their objective for dating. Is it just to have fun? Is this about having a friend with benefits? Or do they value monogamy and want marriage? Believe it or not, having this conversation will be a great conversation starter and you will learn lots from the date by asking this simple question.

The bottom line is, if your desire is marriage that's no reason to be ashamed. If you ask this question, it doesn't mean you are saying you want to get married tomorrow or even have a timeframe in mind. This question just simply sets the tone for where the relationship is headed. Someone with serious intentions will not mind your being up front and will appreciate your candor.

Most of the time, however, we do the opposite. We get to know the person first. That is, we become aware of their likes, dislikes, where they grew up, their heritage, who their mother is and what they like to do in their free time. Then once you have fallen in love with the idea of being with this person, because it certainly isn't love yet, it makes it harder to break away when they tell you that they are just having fun. Wait what??? All this time we just spent together and you want to have fun. This behavior is what causes people to stay in relationships that are not going anywhere. They get used to the person and feel that they can change them if they are just patient and wait it out. Listen, the odds are against you. You are simply settling and that's not okay. There is somebody out there for you, but you can't be desperate and expect to attract them. Besides, even if the person comes around eventually, by the time this happens, they have lost so much respect for you because you made it obvious that you would be willing to do nearly anything to have them, even when it means being unhappy yourself.

IN REAL TIME

The last aspect of "Dating SMART" is doing it in real time. According to Merriam-Webster, doing something in real time means the actual time during which something takes place. In other words, as it comes in! You have got to learn to date and share your affection as it comes to you, not as you chase after it. Being successful at dating involves being a whole person prior to involving someone else in something that is not complete. It's almost like inviting someone someplace and not having all the details worked out. Has that ever happened to you? If so, how did that make you feel? Were you frustrated, maybe irritated? Did you wonder why they didn't get their plans together before involving you? Well the same can be said in life when we involve other people in our unfinished process. How unfair! You have got to make sure you are bringing a potential mate to something complete and defined, not chaotic. If you don't know what you want, then they sure won't be able to tell you. Your individual identity or value cannot be tied to the success or failure of a relationship. Sometimes we date with the intention of marriage because we are unhappy with who we are as a person and we think getting involved with someone else is going to make that better. Let me tell you, this will only make it worse. You will end up dragging that person down a path that they were not prepared to go.

I dated someone in college and he told me he didn't want to be girlfriend and boyfriend, but he enjoyed spending time with me. I also enjoyed spending time with him, and because of how we were with one another, I settled for not having a title because I had him, or at least that's what I thought. However, not having a title gave me no leverage when I found out how he was cheating on me with someone else. Well, was he really cheating because we weren't official but were suppose to be doing exclusive things, if that makes sense. I spent nearly three years of my life doing all sorts of things for this guy hoping that he would come around one day and change his mind to make our relationship official.

I lost myself during this time period by constantly changing into what I thought he wanted me to be because I was so desperate to be in a relationship. Since no one else was beating my door down I felt like I needed to stick with him, I mean it was better than being alone, so I thought. For awhile, we dated even after graduating from college, so the dynamics changed some in

24

our relationship. Now, we were no longer on campus, but two grown people with our own apartments and good entry level jobs straight out of college in our fields. I remember wanting to get to this point because I made excuses in my head throughout college that maybe we would become official after we graduated. I convinced myself the he probably wanted to focus on finishing college before becoming serious. Well, we finished college and still had no commitment. I mean, we were spending lots of time together and doing all the things that couples do but without any strings attached. While this was working for him, it was killing me on the inside. It destroyed my self-esteem and I lost my self-worth. It was nobody's fault but mine. The guy did not do me wrong because he was honest from the beginning. However, I chose to allow my fantasy of a potential "girlfriend" role to override what he was telling me all along and that was, he didn't want to be in a committed relationship. He was just "kicking it." I said I was good with something that my heart just couldn't take. It wasn't until after graduation that I was introduced to my husband and I finally cut ties and decided to move on, taking a chance at finding true love.

My purpose in sharing this with you is so that you will realize your self-worth early and not tie that to anyone. You will meet many people, some you will click with and some maybe not so much. But no matter what happens DO NOT base your value as a person on what happens in those relationships. I want you to get a plan for dating, find out what the other person's intentions are and BELIEVE, what they tell you. Why don't we believe people when they tell us how they truly feel? It is as if we say "okay" in our minds and then proceed to wait it out in hopes we can change them. Absolutely not!! If you have ever done this, please don't do this again! You CANNOT change a grown person. Did you hear that? YOU CANNOT CHANGE A GROWN PERSON! I have learned the only way a person can change is with God.

CHAPTER TWO NOTES:

CHAPTER TWO:
Reflection & Application

1. What are you looking for in a relationship and why are you dating?

_____
_____
_____
_____
_____
_____
_____
_____
_____
_____

2. Share how you honestly explained or will explain your intentions to the person you are dating. Why is it important to discuss intentions?

_____
_____
_____
_____
_____
_____
_____
_____
_____
_____

CHAPTER THREE

So You Think You've Found the One?

*N*ow that you know how to date let's talk about finding "the one". In our Western culture we often hear people say that they have found "the one". When you hear this what do you think they mean? For most, they mean they have found their soulmate; the one they were intended or destined to be with all along. For others, it means the right person or the one with whom they are most compatible.

I do not personally subscribe to the idea of soulmates because it perpetuates the notion that you are only destined to be with one person and when you find this person you must make the relationship work despite all odds. If you feel that there is only one person in the entire universe with whom you can be fruitful and multiply - God's first command, then you will settle and perhaps stay in something that is not healthy because you feel there is no other option. This idea has caused many people to stay in toxic situations as they work to downplay their partner's weaknesses and magnify strengths in order to justify the relationship (Jet, 2003).

The term soulmate is rooted in ancient Greek Mythology. It was be-lieved that in the beginning humans were split in half as punishment for angering the gods. After the split, mankind was doomed to search for his/her missing half (Todeschi, 1999). The idea is that there's only one person that will perfectly fit your missing half and you must search to find them in order to be whole again (Todeschi, 1999). This is probably why some people say their significant other completes them. However, there is no real proof for this theory. As you date you need to know that you must bring 100 percent into the relationship. If you are bringing any less than that, sit on the bench for a while.

As stated earlier, dating is still not even a universal practice. In many cultures, relationships are arranged by parents who vet possible mates that they feel are well-suited for their children. After doing so, the two young people are introduced to one another and given time to get to know each other for the sole purpose of marriage. In these arrangements, couples are forced to grow in love, meaning love was not there when they married. So what was there? Perhaps one of the other major elements that makes a marriage successful, COMPATIBILITY, which we will discuss a little later in this chapter.

I believe God will bless a union between two people who are willing to put Him first, ask Him for guidance and do the work to make the relationship great. I don't believe that there is only one person in the entire world that you could be married to and have a thriving relationship. From my perspective, the bible does not support this.

If you look in the bible, you will not find any evidence of soulmates. As a matter of fact, the first directive to Adam and Eve in the book of Genesis was to be fruitful and multiply. Thereafter, people united in marriage to do this, many times from the same family as the earth was not well populated. Am I saying that you need to marry your cousin? Of COURSE NOT! However, I am saying that the institution of marriage in the bible was not based on soulmates. It was rather about joining lives with someone to reproduce. The Old Testament Scripture below provides an example of an arranged marriage, with great influence from the parents as to the family or community the potential spouse should come.

> One day Abraham said to his oldest servant, the man in charge of his household, "Take an oath by putting your hand under my thigh. Swear by the LORD, the God of heaven and earth, that you will not allow my son to marry one of these local Canaanite women. Go

instead to my homeland, to my relatives, and find a wife there for my son Isaac." The servant asked, "But what if I can't find a young woman who is willing to travel so far from home? Should I then take Isaac there to live among your relatives in the land you came from?" "No!" Abraham responded. "Be careful never to take my son there. For the LORD, the God of heaven, who took me from my father's house and my native land, solemnly promised to give this land to my descendants. He will send his angel ahead of you, and he will see to it that you find a wife there for my son." (Genesis 24:2-5, NLT)

This account is about the marriage of Isaac to Rebekah. Abraham told his servant where to find a wife for Isaac and gave specific instructions on from where she should come. Although the marriage was arranged by Isaac's parents, God honored it because not only did Abraham speak with assurance that an angel would go ahead of the servant for direction, but the servant also prayed to God to show him which woman he should take back for Isaac.

"O Lord, God of my master, Abraham," he prayed. "Please give me success today, and show unfailing love to my master, Abraham. See, I am standing here beside this spring, and the young women of the town are coming out to draw water. This is my request. I will ask one of them, 'Please give me a drink from your jug.' If she says, 'Yes, have a drink, and I will water your camels, too!'—let her be the one you have selected as Isaac's wife. This is how I will know that you have shown unfailing love to my master." Before he had finished praying, he saw a young woman named Rebekah coming out with her water jug on her shoulder. She was the daughter of Bethuel, who was the son of Abraham's brother Nahor and his wife, Milcah. Rebekah was very beautiful and old enough to be married, but she was still a virgin. She went down to the spring, filled her jug, and came up again. Running over to her, the servant said, "Please give me a little drink of water from your jug." (Genesis 24:12-17, NLT)

If you are thinking about dating, or are dating right now, you need to do it intentionally. I encourage you to seek God for direction just as this servant did for Isaac before connecting too deeply, especially if your desire is marriage. If left to your own methods, you may not choose wisely and pick someone solely based on superficial reasons. When you put God first and ask him for direction, you will never go wrong. Your path will be clear from the start and you will save yourself lots of time and potential heartache. Allow God to do the arranging and vet out the person that will work best for you.

So instead of finding a soul mate, maybe you should pray to God to put the person in your path that is most compatible for you. What is compatibility? According to Merriam-Webster Dictionary, it means capable of existing together in harmony. When it is all said and done, you need to be in a relationship that is harmonious with as few issues as possible. What generally causes the most issues in relationships? Our differences! In my experience working with clients, I have found that there are two main areas that drive compatibility which, in turn, makes reaching harmony possible:

A Person's Past

Many people enter relationships blind, having no idea of the other person's past. We can be so desperate at times to be in the relationship that we fail to ascertain the answer to the most important question—where did this person come from? In order to know where a person is going, you must understand where they have been. The way a person proceeds through life, the risks they choose to take, as well as the choices they make, all come from learned behavior and values instilled in them. Conversely for others, it's a lack of values that will be problematic for the relationship.

A really bad childhood experience can also produce more of the same into adulthood OR push a person to change for the better. When you date someone, with the intention of marrying that person, it is important to gather as much information as possible before getting too serious. Obviously, this is so that you can make the best decision for such a life-changing event. I mean it is the rest of your life!

I grew up in a two-parent home and my husband grew up in a single parent home. Growing up, both of my parents were heavily involved in every aspect of my life, while Bruce only had his mother because his father was nowhere to be found. My mindset was different just because I had a father in the home. I regarded certain things as normal because I watched how my parents did them. I adopted certain roles for what I believed the wife should do versus the husband because that is what I saw. However, Bruce did not

32

have that vantage point. He saw his mother do it all and that was simply foreign for me. While Bruce and I both shared many of the same basic values, with such differences in our upbringing, we had to figure out the roles and expectations we would have for our new family. Unfortunately, this didn't happen until we were already married. We had to identify a middle ground on what to anticipate from each other and how we would work together as a couple.

Cultural differences, as it relates to someone's past, can also be so big that you can't agree on what works for the relationship. In many Eastern cultures, the wife has little to say in the business of the marriage or in final decisions. Certain religions can also dictate this. If you date someone from a different culture you need to ask certain specific questions. Is value placed on the husband *and* wife's opinions or are final decisions usually left to the husband? Do you believe in monogamy or do you come from a polygamist family? These are just a few of the many questions that must be asked and issues that must be addressed. This is why it is imperative to find out as much as possible about your partner's culture and religion while dating.

I have even seen women misinterpret their partner's domineering nature as a sign of thoughtful caring only to discover a much bigger problem down the road. I remember being out to dinner with some girlfriends years ago and witnessing this first hand. My friend thought that it was cute how her man continued to call and text her while we were out, "just to check in". In my mind I wondered why he needed to check in so many times when he knew where she was and who she was with. Why couldn't he allow her to enjoy time with her friends for the evening? I believe this behavior was based on his past insecurities that he brought into their relationship.

A Person's Personality

The intrinsic things that make a person who they are determines how they interact with the world and how they engage in relationships. It is our inherent flaws that our mate gets a front row seat to: often invisible to the outside world. The fact is, we all prefer to spend the most time with people who we get along with best. Unfortunately, there is no perfect, cookie cutter relationship. The relationships portrayed in magazines and movies are not real. What is real is the fact that any relationship worth having will involve work. The level of work is going to be dependent upon how compatible you are with your mate. Remember, the less compatible you two are, the more work you will have to put into the relationship.

Harmony will be more important in your day-to-day dealings with your mate than whether they graduated from an Ivy League school or have millions of dollars in the bank. We tend to spend time with people whom we get along with because we are naturally drawn towards them, given similar personality traits. You will need this "draw" when things get tough in your relationship so don't ignore it.

Don't Knock It Until You Try It

Over the years I have come to realize that compatibility will not always jump out at you. It won't always be wrapped up in a nice pretty little bow as you might think. You might like your man tall, dark and handsome, but compatibility might be in a short, light-skinned, average looking man. On the flipside, you might want your woman to be a Brickhouse, 36-24-36 but the best compatibility for you might be a 42-35-52. The point is not to dismiss someone just because they may not be ideal in your sight. What's ideal to us is usually based off learned expectations imposed upon us by those we hold in high esteem. Whether it is how someone should look, how many degrees they have or their accomplishments. In the end, it is important to separate what truly works for you from what others think will work. The point is, don't knock the idea of dating someone just because they don't fit your profile until you try it.

Many feel that compatibility requires a couple to share the same interests or like the same things in order for their relationship to work but this couldn't be farther from the truth. There is an old adage that says, "opposites attract", which is very true. We tend to be attracted to the person who brings out the attributes in us that we wish we had or that we lack. If a person wants to be with someone who they don't have much in common with then that's certainly their prerogative. However, you need to know up front that doing so increases the probability that there will be issues later. The couple will likely have to work harder at connecting in certain ways. On the other hand, connecting may come naturally to those who share common interests and ideals about the world that we live in. Just remember, the wider the gap of common ground, the more work will be involved to create harmony and connection. This work is called compromise.

CHAPTER THREE NOTES:

_____

_____

_____

_____

_____

_____

_____

_____

_____

_____

_____

_____

_____

_____

_____

_____

_____

_____

_____

_____

_____

CHAPTER THREE:

Reflection & Application

1. Do you believe in soulmates? Why or Why not? How do you know you have found "the one"?

_____

_____

_____

_____

_____

_____

_____

_____

2. List 2 areas where you feel you and your partner are not naturally compatible? How can you overcome this challenge?

_____

_____

_____

_____

_____

_____

_____

_____

_____

CHAPTER FOUR

Learning to Compromise

*U*nderstandably, people naturally gravitate toward those with whom they are most compatible. Compatibility helps couples co-exist with little issues because they complement one another even in their differences. Compromise, on the other hand, helps you appreciate the other person's differences and adapt when it's not naturally organic for you to do so. The most important thing to remember is even if you and your significant other have different upbringings, past experiences, likes and/or dislikes, you can still agree to a new standard as long as you both agree to compromise where needed. Relationships are not one-sided and will be filled with times of one partner backing down and the other standing up, or times when both are pulling and pushing for their right to be heard or to have their way. At times, some of you will be backing down because it's not worth the argument and others of you will be standing up because you believe so strongly in your position. Just remember that simply because you grew up a certain way does not mean it is absolute and the only right way. Your significant other could have a different way, just as valid as your own.

Trying To Fit In

You cannot say you love someone and want the best for them and not be willing to do what is necessary in order to make life easier for them. This involves allowing them to feel comfortable in their own skin and not expecting them to change like a chameleon just to be with you. The interesting thing about chameleons is their ability to adapt to their environment in order to survive. They can change the color of their skin to blend in or to stand out. Have you ever adopted "chameleon like" ways to stand out to a potential mate, tone it down when maybe your personality was too loud or even change to intimidate someone else. Whether we want to admit it or not, most of us have done this in some variation or form at some point in our lives. As humans we know how to adapt to our environment. The danger is when this changing becomes a part of who we are and our mechanism to fit in with certain people or even to engage in romantic relationships. This often means you are not comfortable with yourself nor do you believe people will accept you for being you. Therefore, you end up trying to become who you think your partner wants you to be.

In the past, I have been in both romantic and platonic relationships and knew that I was not being true to myself. Before long, I found myself saying some of the same little phrases my partners and friends said, wearing the same things they wore, and being interested in some of the things they liked; all of which I had no desire for prior to meeting them. When we don't know ourselves and who we are, we will totally change, not simply compromise. Recognize that there is a difference! As you seek to find that special someone, I don't want you to totally change who you are unless you know you have a bad habit or personality trait that you need to break or change for you. On the contrary, if you happen to have a certain way of doing things, love a particular past time or have a value or tradition that's been passed down, don't just stop doing it all together simply because it's not your significant other's interest. Instead, this is where compromise comes in for both of you, which may entail some stretching and adapting on both parts.

I have often heard people say that when you date, you send your representative, not the real you. What this means is that you are careful not to show what may be the undesirable side of your persona. You put your best foot forward in order not to scare off a potential mate. Instead, you choose to keep the secret, only to reveal it once the paperwork (marriage license) is signed. I want to encourage you not to do this because this is manipulation. If you have some weird habit or like something that you think your partner is not going to support, be up front about it. Don't get married and once the ink dries, tell your spouse something that you know he or she is going to have a hard time accepting. Compromise starts in the dating phase and will continue throughout marriage as the two of you are exposed to new friends, new places and new experiences. You will have to constantly talk about your likes and dislikes as you decide your new normal as a couple. So, to lessen the shock, try to get as many known differing views on the table before marriage and commit to some type of resolve or plan for compromise. Trust me, once you are married you will have enough new stuff to adapt to for a lifetime.

Our Compromise

When I work with couples, one of the main things we talk about is roles and expectations in their relationship. How one defines these often stems from what each person witnessed growing up. In my household as a child, we had dinner pretty much every day around 5:30pm. We were told to go and wash our hands and everybody sat around the dinner table together. My mother fixed our plates most of the time. Even if she didn't fix plates for my sister and me, she always served my dad. Once our plates were on the table, no one started eating until everyone was seated. My dad generally said the grace or blessing over the meal and then we ate. Of course, there were no electronics at the table, because at that time, there were no electronics period!! So, that temptation was not there as it is today for many families. Therefore, you will need to decide what your family rule or tradition will be as it relates to shared time and electronics. But back to mealtime, if the television was on, it was likely turned to the local news. We discussed our day and had intelligent conversations with our parents. If we wanted to leave the table, we asked to be excused before just getting up. When dinner was over, my sister or I generally cleared the dishes and cleaned up the kitchen.

Now when Bruce and I got married, after I finished cooking, I would let him know dinner was ready and he would come into the kitchen to get his plate. Now if he was watching something on television or playing his X-box at the time, then that is where he returned to eat, once he got his plate. I didn't understand his procedure because this was foreign to me and not the way I was raised. However, I didn't really say much about it because my parents never allowed us to eat anywhere else in the house except at the table. Growing up, I always said when I got my own place, I was going to eat all over the house; in the bedroom and living room. I guess some part of me felt like I was rebelling and got satisfaction out of doing it that way.

So years went by with us doing our own thing. Sometimes we ate together, sometimes we didn't. Although I was enjoying this new found freedom as an adult, something still just didn't seem right. It wasn't until we had Simone and she was old enough to sit at the table with us, that it became important to me, to have family meal time. I had not pushed the issue before because I kinda liked what we were doing. I enjoyed the flexibility, but later I saw how important it was to be together at mealtime. We were missing important time to connect and share our day. I wanted to recreate the experience that I had growing up, of family eating together at the table. It was not until Bruce and I had a conversation about this that I understood why he didn't really do this. It was in no way to disrespect me. Bruce didn't know that sitting together at mealtime was even important to me. He didn't think it made me feel alone at times when he returned to his mancave to eat his food. In his household, everybody grabbed their food and went wherever they wanted to eat; which may have been in front of the television, in the living room or even on a bed. They did not sit down together, to eat as a family at a table on a daily basis.

So, we talked about it and while he didn't experience this growing up, he agreed it was important. We then started slowly working at eating together more and breaking the temptation to go off and do our own thing as we had done so often. In our first house, you could not see the television from the kitchen so when we sat down to eat; we were forced to talk to each other. Even for me, it felt awkward. Growing up, when we sat down to eat together, the television was still in view and I realized that I enjoyed having something on while eating. So Bruce and I had to come up with how things would be in our home and not exactly like it was in either of our childhood homes. Today, we eat as a family as much as we can. We have come up with our own tradition; our way and what works best for us. It is a cross between the flexibility he was used to and the rigidity that I experienced. It doesn't look exactly the same mainly because our work schedules at times impedes us from eating together; but we try to make it a priority as much as we can. However, if for some reason we are all home and not interested in eating at the same time, that is okay too! We just do our thing. This is just an example of a tradition or value you might have that shouldn't be lost if it is something really important to you. Whether or not your spouse shares the same values, doesn't make your way right and their way wrong. You have to decide what "your" family will do and be open to trying things a new way and adapting to your new environment while staying true to who you are.

Shared Time

Shared time is going to be important in your marriage relationship. So the amount of time that you continue to devote to that favorite pastime or hobby is going to be dependent on how much you both are willing to bend. I want you to keep this phrase in mind, "shared activity breeds connectivity." Why do I say that? Generally, the more time you spend with a person, the more you connect on a deeper level because you see a different side to them in various shared situations that maybe you would not have seen had you not experienced it with them. The more time you spend with a person you begin to see their likes and dislikes, what gets them excited, what angers them and even what disappoints or saddens them. Shared activity is so important and becomes a big area of compromise if you want to enhance your marriage and deepen your relationship.

No matter your preference, whether you enjoy shopping, hiking, going to the opera, bowling or hunting; these all involve you going someplace. So, the rate at which you will be able to continue doing these things will be dependent on how much shared time your significant other is willing to invest with you doing them. I know, I know, you are probably saying, I need "me time" and that is absolutely correct; you do need "me time" in marriage. You need time to connect with friends of the same gender and you need time to connect with your significant other as well. I am not talking about that. Rather, the enormous amount of time that some people spend hanging out with their friends, enjoying a favorite pastime, hobby or activity that separates them from their significant other: seemingly, ALL THE TIME! I want to caution you here that this will cause conflict in your relationship, at some point or another.

I know a couple who was married for 25 years. I never saw them do much of anything together as a couple. They had one child and after they put that child through school, their relationship completely fell apart. You know why? They had not built up their shared time! They were both so involved with their own pastimes and the detriment to their relationship was masked very well because they were connected for the sake of raising their child together. Raising children requires communication, so they had that down pat as they went to events together that were centered around the child. But when the child left the home, there was no foundation of connectivity. It was so awkward for them to stay together; it was like living with a total stranger as they had both evolved into different people over the years. Sadly, they divorced! I want to caution you not to allow this to happen; as this is the unfortunate story of so many couples.

So where does compromise come in? I am glad you asked, right here! The person who has the hobby will need to compromise if they are spending too much time engaging and the other person will need to compromise by involving themselves in their partner's activity from time to time if it is not already something that they like doing. Again, I say, you have to think "we" not just "me" when you get married. If you don't want to consider someone else's feelings or check in with them to see if they are good with what you are doing, then just stay single. Marriage is not for you! Think of it this way; there are so many things in life that we do separately from our significant other. Many of us work separately and spend longer awake periods of time with those we work with than with the people in our household. If you figure the average person works from 9am to 5pm and sleeps 8 hours a night, that is 16 hours out of 24 hours that we are not actively spending with our mate. Now, mind you, that is a traditional schedule, what about the people whose spouses work 12 hour shifts, which cuts even deeper into the 24 hours. So, I said all of that to say, you have to spend what's left very wisely and be intentional in your planning.

There will be times when your significant other will ask you to do something that's just not you; it goes against your inherent temperament. You just don't like it as it goes outside of your set of interests and that's okay, I get that. For an example, no one is saying that you have to go camping every weekend if you absolutely hate the outdoors, but how will you compromise if your mate loves nature and feels most at peace when outdoors? Is it fair for them not to do what makes them happy because they are now with you? Is it fair for you to be left behind, at home every weekend alone, because you don't enjoy what they like? Absolutely not! In this situation if the person who likes camping loves doing it rugged, with a tent, out in the middle of nowhere, with no shower and no running water, maybe they compromise by upgrading the experience from a traditional campground from time to time to a "glamping" experience, which just means camping with some amenities and resort-style services. Remember, the goal is to try to slowly break your partner into liking what you like so you might have to pull out all the stops to make them feel comfortable. If you are willing to do this, I am sure it would be much appreciated and you will have a better chance at them coming along than if you took them out in the middle of nowhere and expected them to deal with it.

Remember, we all naturally gravitate toward people who celebrate us, understand us and are interested in the things we are interested in. This is why it is so important to study your mate. Get to know what they like or dislike and try to show your support as much as you can. I'm not saying that if they love going to the drag strip and hearing loud cars race up and down the track, you have to go all the time or if they like shopping all day you have to follow them around to every store in the mall to show you care. However, do have an open mind and try to show some interest from time to time. If that means going with them periodically for the sake of you spending time together, then do so.

Like I said previously, my husband is an introvert and tends not to be very demonstrative. This has been an issue for us, on and off throughout our marriage. I am very expressive and him not being that way comes across at times as "unconcerned." I wanted so badly for Bruce to show me his expressive side because I knew it had to be there. Sometimes, I would run into the house excited to tell him something, only to get an, "oh, ok then" as his reaction. Anybody else been there? While he is low-key about a lot of things, there is one thing that gets him riled up and fully expressive...UNC Tarheel Basketball! Anybody that knows my husband knows that he is a UNC fanatic. He has our loft area totally "baby- blued" out. If you are ever trying to think of a great gift to give him, just get him something with the Tarheels on it and you will be good! Now, like I said, he is mostly reserved. However, if he is watching a game, he will be up out of his seat, yelling, even screaming at the television screen as if Roy Williams and the other players can hear him. With sports, I will see a whole entire range of emotions from him that nothing else in this world seems to spark. He absolutely loves sports, particularly basketball. So, I know where to find him when basketball season starts, right on the couch in front of the big screen! I love that he has stayed true to the fact that he likes sports as it has encouraged me to even watch and attend basketball games with him. I am not much of a sports person, but I know it is important to my husband and I enjoy seeing that other side of him demonstrated and engaged. The point is, to reap the benefits of shared activity, sometimes it will involve you doing something that you might not be that excited about. Even though it might not be your thing, if you truly love the person, seeing the pure joy that it brings them is priceless. Trust me, if you show interest in something that your significant other knows you don't particularly care for but are doing for them, even if they don't admit it, your actions go a long way and you will see them reciprocated!

CHAPTER FOUR NOTES:

CHAPTER FOUR:

Reflection & Application

1. In order of importance, list the top 3 areas of compromise needed in your relationship.

   _____

   _____

   _____

   _____

   _____

   _____

   _____

   _____

2. What does acceptable support look like for you?

   _____

   _____

   _____

   _____

   _____

   _____

   _____

   _____

   _____

   _____

CHAPTER FIVE

Say What You Mean, Mean What You Say

ave you ever said something to your mate and just as soon as it came out of your mouth you realized it was not communicated correctly? At that point, the awkwardness of trying to retract your foot out of your throat is no easy feat. It is now "in the atmosphere" and there is no turning back. If you were honest, it is most likely because you did not think before you spoke. As you head towards marriage, it is going to be imperative that you carefully choose your words. The bible says in James 1:19, *"Wherefore, my beloved brethren, let every man be swift to hear, slow to speak and slow to wrath:"* (KJV). There is a reason why you have two ears and only one mouth. Maybe it is to hear double the amount of what you speak. However, if we were honest, we probably do just the opposite. We talk way more than we listen and even when we listen, we hear what we want to hear. The art of communication is something to be studied. For we communicate not only verbally but nonverbally through our actions and our body language. Sometimes the non-verbal is more powerful than our words. We jump to conclusions based on the *way* something was communicated and not based on what *was* communicated. Learning this now is going to help you tremendously as you embark upon marriage.

According to H. Norman Wright, there are 6 Messages in Couple Communication:

1. What you meant to say
2. What you actually said
3. What your spouse actually hears
4. What your spouse thinks you said
5. What your spouse says about what you said
6. What you think your spouse said about what you said

I think many of us find ourselves stuck someplace within numbers 1 to 3 never really discovering number 6. What we meant to say and what we actually said never quite translates to what our mate hears. This is because of all the extra body language. You might say, well I did not say it! Well, you did not have to because your gestures and facial expressions gave the answer.

Let me give you a scenario. You are really annoyed because for weeks you have asked your mate to help you with something you need to get done and they "seemingly" have not found the time. To you it feels like they are prioritizing everything and everyone above you and what you need. You have been walking around not addressing it because you are playing games, attempting to test their commitment and loyalty to you by waiting for them to bring it back up. Surely, if they care and you are a priority they should remember. Right? In a haste, without thinking, you go off as you hear them making plans to do something else and you say, "I guess I'm not important!" Immediately your significant other turns to look at you and says, "Huhhh?" totally caught off guard by your outburst. You have been working your way up to this, letting your thoughts get the best of you, internalizing everything they do, certain that their inability to do what you asked is somehow directly connected to how they feel about you. Yet, it never crossed your mind that perhaps they simply forgot. Or maybe it did cross your mind but because you always remember things that are priority for you, you judge them and draw the conclusion that you are not a priority for them like they are to you, because it slipped their mind. Do you see how convoluted that just got? The entire situation could have been solved had you come back and mentioned, "Don't forget, I need your help with..." to proactively remind your significant other.

Now I know there are instances where the person has not forgotten, and they are just selfishly not doing what you have asked. In which case, something much deeper is brewing that should probably be addressed in a session, so come see me! However, for the sake of this conversation, what if they truly just forgot? You spent all that time conjuring up thoughts in your head that were not real. Maybe they were tired when you asked or maybe your timing was just off. Getting the correct response in your relationship is all about timing. You must study your significant other to know when you should communicate certain things, ask them for things, and expect to have deep conversations. The reaction or response you receive back will depend on timing. You have to stop with the negative self-talk and sabotage; always thinking that someone does not have your best interest at heart, leaving little room for mistakes. Don't be so critical. This tends to happen when you have experienced consistent, repeated negative behaviors in past relationships or even in your current one. You have got to learn to view each situation objectively and not subjectively as you prepare for marriage.

Fighting Fair

Many times, we enter relationships very defensively, constantly needing to prove our point, opinion, or perspective. Where does this come from? Maybe it comes from not being heard in other places like work, church, other groups or perhaps past romantic relationships or even platonic friendships. Anytime you have felt like your opinion was not heard or better yet, devalued, it will cause you to act defensively. You will do whatever you need to do to find control in whatever situation you can get it in. For me, it was in my marriage. To everyone else on the outside, I was the non-assertive person who generally went along for the sake of keeping the peace, but in my marriage, I wanted the last word. It was going to be done my way, somehow. In the early phase of our marriage, I acted like a spoiled brat. The relationship I was in right before meeting my husband had left me feeling devalued. I carried that baggage into our marriage. Unknowingly, I went into the marriage with a chip on my shoulder, determined that my husband would not get over on me and that I would assert myself this time around. Many times I jumped to conclusions that were not accurate.

If we learn to relax, knowing that our significant other is on the same side we are on, it will make life so much easier. You must both go after the

53

win; not the individual win but the collective win. Creating moments that you win in understanding each other, win in fighting for each other's feelings, win in protecting each other's peace and win in creating a space for your mate to grow into a better version of themselves, is what REALLY matters most!

Moments are intervals of time that you will never get back. They are here one second and gone in an instance. So, the question becomes how best to spend these moments while dating for marriage. Your goal should be to use moments wisely to avoid the pitfalls that I mentioned. Yes, I think the answer is simple. Approach each moment as if it were your last. I know that sounds cliché, right? Well, it is true. If you thought in the moment of a heated argument it would be your last opportunity to communicate with your significant other, you might choose your words more wisely. Your goal should be to exalt your significant other not tear them down. Perhaps you are reading this, and you realize that you often tear your partner down to make yourself feel better or to make a point in the moment. I challenge you to dig deep to figure out where that comes from and make a conscious effort from this point on to improve. That type of behavior will not sustain a marriage. As a matter of fact, it's one of the fastest ways to drive your partner into the arms of someone else. Do not take your significant other for granted, feeling as though they will always be there or that they cannot find anyone else to replace you. Thinking that way is arrogant. Arrogance does not concede, and it does not submit. Arrogance also feels like it can do or say anything when it gets backed into a corner or is challenged.

Many times, early in my marriage, arrogance came across from both of us in the undertones of our arguments. We both wanted to win the argument, not realizing that marriage is not a sprint but rather a marathon. What you are building in marriage is so much more than just in the moment of a disagreement. Growing up you probably heard the phrase, "Sticks and stones may break my bones, but words will never hurt me". Well, that is one of the biggest lies ever told! Words do hurt and once they are out of your mouth you cannot get them back. In an argument, I could cut so smooth that you would not even realize I just cut you until thinking about it later. It was not until I did a lot of self-reflection that I realized I was wrong and that my words had power. I was broken and insecure which came across in how I communicated with my husband in the beginning of our marriage. I did not want to submit to my husband's leadership of our household. At the time, I really felt I was more mature in certain areas and I thought things should be done a certain way. This is another reason why you need to make sure you are bringing 100 percent into the relationship and not 50 percent, waiting for your significant other to match it. Two halves do not make a whole. Two halves make a mess!

Problem Now, Problem Later

Sometimes when issues present themselves while dating, couples disregard them and pledge to work on them after marriage. However, this is the wrong mindset to have. You must know that if something is a problem now, without intervention, it will be a problem later. Resolving issues does not get easier after marriage. As a matter of fact, it gets harder because everything you did while dating to keep them, goes out of the window. Once you are married, the need to impress comes to a screeching halt because both of you will be more comfortable and will settle into who you really are. As a result, I do not agree with couples living together before marriage. Some couples choose to live together prior to marriage because they say they want to give things a "test run". They move in together desiring to learn more about the person they feel they might want to spend the rest of their lives with. But trust me, even if you live together before marriage, you will still discover new things after marriage. The reality is, people are not going to be honest until they are forced to be, if they are truly hiding something. I say all of that from experience because my husband and I lived together for about six months before we got married.

Shortly after we got engaged, he had to figure out what he was going to do with his lease, so it seemed like a good decision for him to move in with me. Not only were we trying to save up for our wedding and honeymoon, but we were having a house built during our engagement and needed to put away money for the closing. However, living together really did not prove useful. I remember being more reserved in my actions and reactions because I was trying to impress him. I do not feel like I truly expressed all of me until we were married. I do not know if this had a lot to do with the fact that we were under each other so much and I did not have the opportunity to process things or what. I just know that there were many issues that I suppressed and thought in my head that we had a lifetime to work on them, so why deal with them now? Little did I know that once we married, we would both settle more firmly into who we really were, just to dig our heels even more deeply in the proverbial sand. Our inability to resolve conflict during our dating and engagement led to some of the major issues we experienced early on in marriage. We did not know how to fight fair or how to agree to disagree. One important aspect of any relationship is to understand that you both are on the same team. When you come into a relationship with this understanding it changes your stance from the start. But remember, we only had one pre-marriage counseling session, so we had not been taught anything about conflict resolution. In my mind it was about proving a point and winning to show that I was right.

PREP First

Even with all the prompting and careful approaches, conflict in relationships is something we all encounter. It is uncomfortable, but we must learn how to deal with it. If we are honest, there are often underlying issues that drive current conflict. So, during my coaching I came up with a strategy to deal with it. This strategy is called "PREP". We prep before doing a lot of things in life. One example that most of us have done is prepping before cooking a meal. Many recipes will include cook time and "prep" time showing that this is one important step that should not be overlooked. Can you cook without prepping, certainly? However, taking the time to prep before cooking makes it easier because it gives you an opportunity to get all the ingredients needed to make sure that everything is measured out exactly right. Doing this ahead of time increases the chances of success because once you start cooking there is no time to be running around the kitchen opening the refrigerator, searching the cabinets for items and trying to find pots suitable for the recipe that will fit. Doing this might result in burning the meal. Could you do it this way, maybe, but you take a much bigger chance of ruining the meal!

The same can be said in resolving conflict in relationships; you must prep first. Do not go at it haphazardly. Prepping of any kind simply involves "making ready." So how do I get ready to tackle conflict, I **PREP**. The **P stands for Pause**, which means, take a breather before saying or doing anything that might cause more issues. So, the minute that conflict arises, you hear or feel an argument coming on, do not just spout off with the first thing that comes to mind, but rather pause in the moment. Hear what is being said to gain deeper understanding before opening your mouth. This is especially important to know because lots of times we get caught in the moment of an argument and go from 0 to 100 in a matter of minutes. However, most times, if we just take a few minutes and pause, we can collect ourselves and gather our thoughts. The **R stands for Reflect**, which means consider any previous issues that might be motivating the current conflict. Now this was especially important for me to learn and is still a strategy I use now. Stay on topic and focus. Now is not the time to drag in what your mate did the other day, last week, the month prior or even the year before. Stay focused on the issue at hand! Make sure you are not making today's issue about something else from the past. It is imperative to separate old stuff from *now* stuff.

As an example, if you are upset at your significant other for not talking to you about an important decision that you feel should have been discussed between the two of you first, you cannot bring up the fact that last week they did something else that made you mad as well and join the two together because that is going to escalate the situation. You should have addressed the previous issue when you had it. In the heat of *the now* conflict is not the time for discussing compounding issues. If you have some major things that are creating unrest for you, that needs to be a sit-down discussion that is planned where you both agree to discuss the hard issues. At that time, go through your list but for now you must only address the *current* conflict in the heat of the moment or argument. Remember, this should not take all day: nor should it be a blood bath. I am trying to get you some resolve, so let us keep going. You must stay focused on the issue at hand.

The **E stands for Examine**, which means assess your current situation to see what the true problem really is. This is where you do some quick mental analysis and ask yourself, "What am I really upset about?" or "What is giving me pause?" In the preceding example, are you mad that your significant other failed to discuss the important decision prior to making it or is the real issue that you feel undervalued and not an equal partner in the relationship? Do you see the difference? In this example, the real issue is that you do not feel that your partner values your opinion and you have decided in your head this is why they did not discuss it with you first. So, both have merit but would be addressed totally differently. Some things can be addressed in the heat of the moment because they are not that big of a deal. You talk about it, share your opinion, and then boom, you are done! Other things must be addressed at a different time when there is more time. Therefore, you need to examine to figure out what the real issue is. I remember, Bruce and I used to get into some deep arguments while traveling in the car which put us in some very awkward situations. We would have just gotten through a heated argument only to pull into the driveway of my grandmother's house on Thanksgiving. For the rest of the day we were bombarded by family; it was a mess. We had to wear fake grins the entire day, pretending we were all good. We eventually learned not to do this. Wisdom and time will help you in knowing when to hold them or when to fold them. You never bring up deep issues when there is not adequate time to deal because somebody's opinion or perspective is going to be cut short and left hanging in the balance and you do not want that.

Lastly, the second **P stands for Proceed**. Having committed to address only the current concern, you may now proceed. Once you have nailed this strategy, it will be easy for you to go through this in your head in a matter of moments and then you can proceed. This will help guide your arguments and help you disagree intelligently with the hopes of gaining better understanding, reaching compromise and ultimately achieving resolve. You can always decide to come back and discuss at a time when things are not heated, when you can give more time or when the atmosphere is right. However, no matter when you choose to address the issue, you have to make sure the discussion is authentic and real. Do not *tip toe* around what is *really* bothering you. Be clear in what you say and state facts. Keep in mind that the outcome should be that you win as a couple. This means that clarity and peace have been brought to the situation and anything less than that is not a win.

You should picture this disagreement much like a surgery, by gently and lovingly approaching the situation. Have you ever played the board game called Operation? In that game you operate on a patient who has lots of different ailments. The object of the game is to try to fix as many of the patient's ailments as possible without touching the sides of his injuries. If you fail to do so you will hear a buzzer go off and you lose your turn. The same approach can be said when trying to have a healthy disagreement with your significant other. The aim should be to pull out as much as you can to resolve the issue without hurting or aggravating anything else.

Chapter Five Notes:

CHAPTER FIVE:

Reflection & Application

1. Identify 2 areas in your relationship in which you "wear a mask" and need to be your authentic self?

_____

_____

_____

_____

_____

_____

2. Why do you think you and your partner argue?
   Do you see patterns? Put your last argument or conflict into the PREP strategy.

_____

_____

_____

_____

_____

_____

_____

CHAPTER SIX

Separating Potential from Reality

My inspiration for this chapter comes from my vantage point as a pre-marriage coach. I have met with couples for coaching, and immediately knew within 5 to 10 minutes of talking to them that they were living in a fantasy world. Not due to a lack of love, commitment or their willingness to try, but rather the status or direction of their individual lives. Couples book sessions all the time in hopes of receiving the tools necessary that will help them mesh their two worlds together yet not actualizing or accepting the reality that they are in two different places desiring very different things out of life. I feel they think there is one exercise or one piece of advice that can be given to help them make it work without doing some very hard sacrificing to make it happen. I urge them not to live heavily in the potential of a situation or person but instead, embrace the reality that stares back at them. Potential is good and we all need it because it is what keeps us aspiring for greater. Without potential you would not go off to college, start that business, write a book, get into a new relationship or simply- **BECOME!**

Having the degree and necessary training in an area is what gives you the potential to succeed in that area. So, I am not saying we don't all operate, at times in our lives, in potential. However, there are some things in life that stare us right in the face that we cannot ignore. These things or obstacles require us to separate the potential of a person or a relationship from the *reality of now*. In a dating relationship headed toward marriage, you should not make life-long commitments solely on potential and promises without seeing some great effort toward that potential or some profits of that potential playing out in your current reality.

As a significant other, it is very important to help your partner realize dreams and strive to become the best person they can be; but at what cost and for how long? When you are dating, there has to be a certain reality for you to stay. You may meet many people who have the potential to do all sorts of things but if they are not on the road to pursuing them as you are dating or have a very valid reason for not doing so, you must make your decision to stay based on what you see now, not what they are dreaming of doing someday. I know, I know, let that settle in and just sit in that truth for a moment. We have all done it from time to time in relationships where we wanted success or opportunities to happen for someone so badly, probably even more than they wanted for themselves. However, when you stand back and look at this picture something is very wrong. You cannot want success for someone more than they want it for themselves, and you must be realistic in assessing their ability to achieve what you want them to achieve. Having a child with someone is not a good reason to stay. There are many people out there being great co-parents without the pressure of trying to be in a relationship with someone when it just doesn't work.

Sometimes we stay in relationships not because we are so in love, but rather because as human beings, we do not like change. Change is uncomfortable and we will stay in bad relationships to avoid this change not realizing that there could be better. I mean, what sense does it make to try to make a relationship work between two people who drive each other absolutely insane? This insanity is bred by the fact that both people want very different things out of life and are headed down two separate paths. Why spend countless hours trying to change someone into something that they are not, when all you have to do is be patient and wait for the person who is most compatible? Remember compatibility brings about harmony. There will be enough things that you will have to work on in your relationship, so connecting yourself with someone who is like-minded is going to be key if you want your path to be smooth.

The bible says in Amos 3:3, *"Can two walk together, except they be agreed?"* (KJV). In other words, you have to be in agreement together in order to be successful together. You cannot pull one way and your partner pull the other way and be fruitful. When I say fruitful, I mean having benefits and profits not only to you as a couple but also to your family and the community around you. Your relationship should be a blessing for others not a burden. Being brutally honest, to recognize whether or not you are in agreement, takes courage. It also takes courage to admit if you are operating in fantasy and not reality. People don't want to admit this, and many times have these light bulb moments after they say, "I do". I encourage you in the dating season of your life to dig deep, clearly distinguish your needs and the needs of your partner so you both live your best life whether that's together or separately.

The Capacity to Embrace Reality

One of the tasks I have on my day job is to help communities that we serve build capacity for projects they want to see funded in their local area. Now what does capacity mean? Capacity is your ability to produce or contain something. For instance, a 12-ounce glass has the capacity to hold 12 ounces of water. It can't hold 20 ounces; it can only contain 12 ounces. It was not made for 20 ounces. A community that wants to hold a summer camp must have the manpower and resources (building, funding, equipment, etc.) available and at their disposal to make that happen or else it does not have the capacity for a summer camp. A business has the capacity to offer homeownership classes to its clients if they have lenders located in that city available and willing to offer loans to individuals living there. Do you get the point; do you see where I am going with this?

Relationships are no different. Lots of times we engage in relationships with people without considering our capacity or ability to accept the realities that come with being connected to that person. Can you be in a relationship with a partner who travels each week for work, leaving you at home to manage the house and kids? Do you have the resources available to support you in doing so? Or, is your schedule demanding as well? If you don't have the support and your schedule is demanding too, without one of you conceding it's just not going to work. You will constantly find yourself arguing about something that was there from the beginning, yet you chose to ignore it.

I was watching a show on television called *Married at First Sight*. These individuals agree to be a part of the show in hopes of being matched by the experts to the person that they are most compatible with on paper. The experts ask many questions, in the interview phase, to make sure they get this right. But there was one particular couple that had an issue with work schedules and travel. Apparently, the female had not made it clear that she did not want a spouse who traveled. After getting married and coming back from their honeymoon, the guy started talking about how he was getting ready to return to work, after taking several weeks off to travel to really get to know her. In that conversation he mentioned traveling for work but did not define what that meant. Turns out he spends several days of each week out of town each month; like almost half the month traveling. Now, for a normal couple who had dated the traditional way, this would be hard, but for the two of them who only knew each other for about 6 weeks, it was detrimental. The female seemed very disappointed and even brought it up as a point of contention to the marriage experts. I think she thought he would look for another job that had a more traditional schedule, but he loved his job and loved what he did and did not seem interested in making any changes anytime soon.

I remember early in our marriage, my husband worked 12 hour shifts with four days on and three days off. Not only were they 12 hour shifts but they also rotated, meaning that sometimes he worked day shifts and sometimes he worked night shifts which put an even more interesting spin on things. It was hard for my husband to get used to the schedule because just as soon as he began to adjust to sleeping in the daytime, it was time to go back to day shift. He did this for probably the first year or so of our marriage and I didn't like it. Thankfully for us, he didn't either and looked diligently for something else and I knew that was the goal from the beginning.

In contrast, just like on *Married at First Sight*, your partner may love their schedule and may not be willing to give it up just because they are marrying you. So, don't be in such a hurry that you ignore the reality that you are getting married only to be spending a lot of time alone. Unless your significant other is planning to change careers or jobs to be with you, these things must be considered seriously before moving forward. Another reality is the fact that, everybody's not going to be an entrepreneur and have their own business. Let me make that clear because sometimes in relationships I have seen both males and females be hard on their mates because they were not grinders like them. Everyone may not desire to hustle and have 3 businesses and that is okay. So, do not make your mate feel bad if he or she does not desire to be an entrepreneur. Some people are not cut out for that because when you work for yourself, you are always working. There is a comfort in knowing that as long as you keep being consistent and showing up every day, there will be a check in the bank at some regular interval. So, there is nothing wrong with enjoying the stability of a company and aspiring to make your way up the corporate ladder. This is why financial conversations are so important early on. If you talk finances you will see how your mate desires to attain wealth.

A Hard Dose of Reality

There is no way I can write a chapter on potential versus reality and not give a hard dose of reality to my ladies for just a moment. Men, please excuse me as I don't mean to be sexist, but I have seen many women stay in relationships with men who they had to "mother", which became a huge liability for them down the road. Now, let me be clear, I think it is noble for you to encourage and uplift your man and push him to greatness as that is your responsibility as a life partner. However, you go too far when you have to do everything for a grown man who has no ambition. Initiative and ambition can not really be taught. In my opinion, either you have it, or you don't. It is hard to unteach laziness. If a person is lazy, that is an inherent trait that they have, that they will have to push through if they even recognize they are that way. When a person is lazy and has no ambition, it breeds contempt in their partner because now their life is being made hard because the partner is not giving 100 percent. Ladies, I urge you strongly to examine the relationship that you are in and if it is with someone who DOES NOT function with ambition and initiative, carefully weigh the costs of staying and decide if it is worth it. If he can't keep a job now, and you do everything for him, just know this will be the narrative for your marriage as well.

Goal Alignment

I have always made a point to get my car aligned every so often but there was a time years and years ago, while I was laid off, that we did not have the money to get it done at the scheduled oil change. The mechanic we

67

used did a free alignment check as part of the oil change service. I remember sitting there in the lobby hoping this was not a time when an alignment was needed. After about 30 minutes the technician came over to me only to confirm my fear that the car did indeed need an alignment. At the time this was going to be an additional $75 that was not in the monthly budget. Now once he said an alignment was needed, I immediately tuned him out because I started thinking through my options. I could decline the alignment and get it done later or make the sacrifice now and move some things around to make it happen. The danger in waiting is that it could cause more problems later and end up costing more money in the end, which is what we wanted to avoid. An alignment helps adjust a vehicle's suspension components to bring wheels and tires into specified angles. These aligned angles help vehicles perform optimally and reduce tire wear.

Sometimes relationships need an alignment of vision and goals to ensure optimal performance. If you have ever looked at an alignment report, it will show if the car is pulling more to the right or left as well as the specific measurements. Maybe in your relationship, one of you are pulling more in an area than the other. Perhaps your goals and dreams shift the relationship to the right and your partner's to the left which throws off the equilibrium of the relationship. You feel out of sorts and things just don't seem to be going straight. When a car has a fresh alignment, you can take your hands off the steering wheel for a while and cruise down the road without steering, as it goes naturally straight on its own. However, when a car needs an alignment, the minute you take your hands off the steering wheel, it begins to pull far right or left. In this instance, someone has to take the wheel or else you will end up in a ditch if you let it continue veering this way. This action can sometimes cause a jerk, which can be an unsmooth ride for passengers. In your relationship, have one of you grabbed the steering wheel suddenly when you saw things going in the ditch which caused some bumps in the road? Some of this can be avoided when you take the time to sit down without reluctance and discuss your dreams, goals and desires.

When I think about what a mechanic has to do to the suspension components to get a car driving straight, I'm sure it requires some bending or twisting. In your relationship, this alignment might mean bending, which is no easy feat especially if you have been used to going a particular direction for a long time. Remember, getting an alignment earlier rather than later is better because more damage is done the longer you allow things to pull unevenly to one side or the other. With a car, there is more likelihood that the tires will need to be rotated and balanced or maybe even replaced which could be costly. What are the costs you're willing to incur by waiting to align yourself with your partner? Remember, we discussed compromise back in chapter four and goal alignment is an extension of the discussion on compromise. Know that the benefit of goal alignment far outweigh the discomfort of making the adjustments now, where necessary before you say, "I do". Take some time and sit down to align your goals now and ask the hard questions so your marriage will be smooth.

CHAPTER SIX NOTES:

_____

_____

_____

_____

_____

_____

_____

_____

_____

_____

_____

_____

_____

_____

_____

_____

_____

_____

_____

_____

_____

_____

_____

_____

CHAPTER SIX:

Reflection and Application

1. Identify one area of your relationship where you have not been realistic. Is it something you have control of? If so, how? Explain how your partner reacts to this area?

_____

_____

_____

_____

_____

_____

_____

_____

2. It's time for an alignment: Identify 2 goals that you know will need to be aligned in your relationship? Here are some areas to consider:
    - Religion
    - Finances
    - Starting a family (or co-parenting)
    - Careers
    - Location of your family

_____

_____

_____

_____

_____

_____

CHAPTER SEVEN

Outside Influences

Many people go toward marriage with the notion that they are just marrying their partner when they are also marrying the people closest to them, including family and friends. There is no way you can expect to marry someone and not be joined to those closest to them as well. I have found that in the dating process, there needs to be just as much vetting of the family and friends, as the person you are dating. You need to know the type of people your significant other chooses to hang around; friends, and the ones that they have been given no choice - family. Knowing the level of influence these people have on your significant other is going to be an important piece for you to consider before heading down the aisle.

Family Dynamics

I know, you may be wondering why you need to vet the family as well, right? Well, here is the reason. Remember, back in chapter four, I talked about the importance of shared time because when you commit you should show interest in the things your significant other likes to do. Well, on an even deeper level, when you commit your life to a person in marriage you also commit to the things that are important to them like family. A person's family dynamics account largely for the person they become in either a positive or negative way. Our behaviors as adults are based in part on things we learned or failed to learn from our family. The things we hold important, many times come from our family.

You need to observe your significant other's relationship with their family. Pay close attention if the relationship is one sided or if it is one of equal give and take. When I say give and take, I mean does there seem to be an equal amount of supportiveness and initiative taken on both ends to make the relationship work? When you are around your significant other, do they always mention having to be the one to take the initiative to call home or go by to see close relatives? Or does it seem to be mutual? On the contrary, does the family have to run your significant other down to get time, attention, or support? If the latter happens without good cause, this could be a reason for pause if your significant other cannot seem to make time for their own family.

I have learned that people make all sorts of excuses, but at the end of the day, we spend time with who we want to spend time with and make relationships a priority that we deem important. The phone rings both ways and the last time I checked there were two sides of every highway to take you in any direction you want to go. Gone are the days of saying you were too busy, or you could not make it happen; people need to admit they choose to do what they want to do. So, the same can be said when it comes to family. If the relationship seems strained on either end, there is something that both sides can do about it to make it better. At any rate, any type of a one-sided relationship is not going to be healthy and will be a strain for the both of you moving forward.

One of the things that is rated and discussed in the *Saving Your Marriage Before It Starts* (SYMBIS) assessment, which is what I use with couples I coach, is a person's independence which is determined by their individuation from their parents (Parrott & Parrott, 2020). This individuation involves their ability to separate from their original family to embrace their new family which is the one you make after you get married. A series of questions are asked throughout the assessment to gauge how much influence everyone allows their family to have over them regarding their life choices. It will be especially important for you to pay close attention to the level of influence your significant other's family has on their choices and their decision-making process or even the lack thereof. This is particularly true when your significant other is so intricately connected with their family, taking much stock in their opinions

74

and or guidance. Just know that if you notice family members having a lot of control over your significant other's decisions, good or bad, this will probably not end automatically simply because you get married.

Now do not misunderstand, I am not saying you should not take the advice of parents or close loved ones. I know my husband and I still do today, even in our relationship. However, advice and opinions have their rightful place. Often people go back and forth with family members to state their opinions where they are not necessary. This is unhealthy and can cause friction between you and your significant other, particularly after you get married. Therefore, you must evaluate the relationship that your significant other has with his or her family early on. As you are dating, observe the type of family your mate comes from. Do they seem to be responsible people? Do they demonstrate sound judgment in their own affairs, and do you truly feel they want the best for your significant other? If you answered "yes" to those questions, while your mate's family members may still insert unsolicited opinions from time to time, at least you know those opinions will be coming from a solid place. However, if your significant other's family is always pulling and in need of something all the time because of poor life decisions, then I would not place too much confidence in what they say.

On the contrary, there could be a severe lack of influence from family and or friends which could cause issues later. If your mate is so stubborn that no one can tell them what to do and they are not willing to listen to sound advice from their parents or family members, then that could be a red flag as well. If they have an estranged relationship with their family, you need to do some research to figure out why. Do not allow them to tell you their side without seeing for yourself. If you find yourself in this predicament, really push to meet and or talk to family so you can draw your own conclusions. I have seen it happen more times than not. People can be whoever they want to be if there is no one around to verify. When a person is willing to enter a marriage relationship without introducing you to their family or consider what their family thinks, this is just as concerning.

At the end of the day, you want the family relationship to be a good one because you are marrying into it. This would also be a great time to evaluate your relationship with your family as well, as this goes both ways. You cannot require something of your mate that you have not taken the time to manage well for yourself with your own family. You do not want to subject your significant other into family dynamics that might be dysfunctional on your end either.

Joining as One

When you get married, everything you do will need to be considered with your new spouse in mind. I believe this is why the bible tells us in Genesis 2:24 *"Therefore shall a man leave his father and his mother and be joined to his wife; and they shall become one flesh"* (KJV). This means that the two should be joined not allowing anyone else to take precedence in the relationship. When you get married you must leave and cleave. Not in a physical way but more so in an emotional way to the extent that you don't allow anyone else to come between you or your new spouse, not a parent, not a sibling, not a best friend, absolutely no one. It is the two of you against the world. You do not allow anyone to speak negatively about your spouse outside of the home. Even if your spouse is wrong, discuss your issues privately with your spouse, AT HOME, between the two of you. Do not allow other people to feel like they can talk about your spouse in front of you. You cannot lend your ear to those things because to be vulnerable with your significant other, you must trust that they have your back. We all go out into the world each day and face all sorts of things but knowing that no matter what, there is at least one person in this world you know you can count on is important. Knowing that you can trust your significant other to have your back even when it comes to differences of opinion within the family is going to be key. Once you establish this and people see the bond you have, they will not even try it.

You will have to figure out what works best for your household and respectfully decline the input of others. If you continue to strive to meet everyone else's expectations all the time, you will not be happy any of the time. Since I turned forty years old, I have concluded that I am no longer going to be uncomfortable to make other people feel comfortable. In other words, if anybody is going to be unhappy in my space, it will not be me. This must be your mantra for your marriage relationship. If anybody is going to be unhappy or uncomfortable, it is not going to be you and your spouse, particularly when it comes to your affairs and how things are done in your household where you pay the bills. If you are still worried about what everyone else thinks, to the extent that you allow it to cause friction in your relationship, then you may need to remain single.

There will be times in marriage when a decision is made to take a new job, to move to another city or even to start a family, and you will not be able to consult all of these different people about what you and your spouse choose to do. It is great to get advice, but do not become paralyzed to the point where you cannot make a sound decision with your spouse because of everyone else in your ear. You must respect the position that your spouse holds as your life partner. You will both be in this thing together and anything less than that is just not acceptable. Now, if you both decide to talk to your parents or consult friends about a situation, then that is fine. However, all of the behind the back, secretive advice seeking, will cause problems every time.

Daddy and Mama Issues

Most of the time, when we hear people discuss "daddy issues" or "mama issues" our brain immediately goes to some type of physical or emotional abandonment, neglect, abuse or trauma. If you or your significant other have dealt with this and have not addressed it, I caution you now to stop and deal with it. Not dealing with those issues now will cause you to project undue expectations and stress on your spouse once you are married; expecting them to be something to you that you lack. So, I want to caution you that if you desire to find a wife with some of your mother's qualities or a husband with some of your dad's qualities, think deeply as to why. Make sure the reasoning is not because you are trying to make your significant other be what your strong mom or dad was to you or what they were not. A husband cannot be your father and a wife cannot be your mother.

On the contrary, there is another "daddy and mama" issue of a different type. When you have been raised by extraordinarily strong parents you can develop a savior or hero mentality that they can do no wrong and create spaces where your new spouse feels they can never measure up. When you have this type of "daddy or mama" issue, you do not know what it is like to be devoid of attention or support. You grow up feeling as though everyone is naturally supposed to congratulate you and support you. But the hard reality is, this world is very cold and while you had amazing parents that shielded you from the ugly parts, it creates this unrealistic view of what relationships will be moving forward.

Girls with strong father figures tend to look for men who possess many of the qualities their dad has. I know from personal experience; I am a Daddy's girl all day. In my mind, growing up, my dad was superman and could do anything. So, imagine getting married to someone half his age, who had not experienced the things my dad had experienced and not had the opportunity to grow and mature in certain areas. I know my dad had to make mistakes growing up as a young man, but I was too young to see them. So, instead of understanding that my new 25-year-old husband at the time could in no way be compared with my experienced 57-year-old father, I placed undue stress on my husband to be someone that he literally could not be at that phase of his life.

Guys with strong mom influences sometimes desire those same qualities in their wives as well. There is nothing wrong with this but understand that you are not marrying your mother. You are marrying another young lady who has been raised by women in her life who instilled their own set of values defining what it means to be a woman. All women are not domestic, and it is unfair to expect your wife to be that. Just because your mom stayed home, kept the house clean, cooked and raised the kids does not mean your wife will want to do this. She may want to have a career and never pick up a broom, mop, or pot. The question is, will you be okay with this? That is why it is so important to talk through roles and expectations early in the dating process and not expect your spouse to be to you, who your parents were.

For an example, imagine loving your mom's cooking and never really giving your wife a chance to cook for the family because you are always bragging or talking about how your mom does it. Now, I am in no way saying ditch mom's cooking! I love my mom's cooking, but you must be sensitive to things that could make your spouse feel uncomfortable as she works to establish a new family with you. Maybe your new wife will do more take-out or prefer to hire a maid to help keep the house clean. In any instance, this will have to be a decision that you both make, not a projected expectation onto the situation. In the cooking example, if your wife wanted to cook, it could make her not even want to try, feeling as though she will never measure up to how your mother does it. While you may want her to have the attributes of your mom that will come in handy one day when you both decide to expand your family, you have got to make sure it is not distended. You should not want to be with someone who mothers you. So, if that is what you are looking for, then you must be honest with yourself that there is something deep down inside of you that is afraid to grow up. Instead of being a man and making your own decisions, you attract women who will be there to tell you what to do which is not your wife's responsibility.

In the end, no matter which type of daddy or mama issues you may have, give your significant other space and room to be their authentic self. If you came from a strong parent with solid attributes, know they did not always have it together and what you see now is a product of years of maturing. On the contrary, if you had a less than desirable experience with your dad or mom growing up, know that your spouse cannot make up for that. Either way, you must do the internal work so not to propel your issues onto your partner. Doing either will cause division and prevent your new spouse from fully assimilating into your family.

What About Your Friends

Now this is a huge one! When it comes to friends made prior to a committed relationship, things can get tricky. Now I am a big proponent for keeping anybody around who has been in your life and made a positive impact prior to you meeting your significant other. HOWEVER, there are some instances that warrant a cut off. First, your friends must understand that you are now married, not still dating. Your spouse is supposed to outrank everyone as it relates to the hierarchy of importance relative to their needs. Your partner needs to know that they come first. So, if your friends cannot understand that and they still infringe upon your privacy and time, then guess what, it might be time to have a talk with them.

I also know of many instances where people have best friends of the opposite sex. Now, me personally, I would not want my husband's best friend to be another female, I do not care if she has been his friend all his life. Not because I am afraid that there could be more to the relationship beyond a platonic nature, but rather the emotional intimacy of best friends. I think past experiences dictate how comfortable you are with friends of the opposite sex. It really depends on the person. Best friends share their deepest secrets and have expectations of one another more so than what they place on others. For me, it is about knowing that there is not another female in this world that connects with my husband the way I do. I want to be the only woman he calls on when in need. So, if you find yourself in this situation and you do not like it, do not pretend to be fine with it only to pitch a fit after marriage. Be up front regarding your expectations of that platonic relationship.

I gave my perspective as a female, but men can have issues as well with their wives having a best friend who is male. Do not be afraid to voice how you feel. Do not fear or worry that it makes you seem jealous or insecure. It does not at all. If the best friend is respectful that you are now coming into the situation and there will obviously be some changes, then proceed ahead if you feel comfortable. However, whether male or female, same sex or opposite sex, if that "best friend" causes issues in the dating relationship by doing things to test your partner's loyalty and your mate does not put them in their place, I say run for the hills. Just know that this is not going to end well and will only get worse after you get married. You will continue to be frustrated that your mate puts their friends wants and needs ahead of yours.

CHAPTER SEVEN NOTES:

_____

_____

_____

_____

_____

_____

_____

_____

_____

_____

_____

_____

_____

_____

_____

_____

_____

_____

_____

_____

_____

_____

_____

_____

_____

CHAPTER SEVEN:
Reflection & Application

1. Identify at least one area where you have allowed your family or close friends to influence an important decision you made that you later regretted. How have you taken steps to prevent this from happening again?

_____

_____

_____

_____

_____

_____

_____

2. Do you feel you have unresolved daddy or mama issues that you are projecting onto your significant other? What is your plan for working through the issue(s) to avoid stressing your relationship with your significant other?

_____

_____

_____

_____

_____

_____

_____

Chapter Eight

So Now What?

We have addressed various topics in this book, from the reasons for dating to practical tips for marriage preparation. Some of the issues discussed may have left you wondering about next steps, and saying, "So now what?". If you are in a committed relationship that is headed toward marriage and you have not considered or had pre-marriage coaching, I urge you to get it now. As you can see from the depictions in the book, there is no benefit to your relationship in waiting. You may not be as familiar with coaching as it is a new concept to some, as pre-marriage counseling has often been the selection for marriage preparation. So, what is the difference between coaching and counseling and which one is best for you?

While there are some similarities between coaching and counseling, there remain differences that distinguish them. *Counseling really focuses on helping a client heal from things in their past that may be causing some type of hurt, pain or distress in their present life. Counseling deals with negative psychology whereas coaching focuses on positive psychology. A coach is not trying to go back to a person's past but instead seeks to walk alongside them in an effort to help them to get to the place they wish to be. Coaching assumes a level of stability that therapy or counseling does not require as people who are looking to be coached have no major problems yet desire more satisfaction in life* (Collins, 2009).

If you seek pre-marriage coaching early in the relationship, at the point you feel marriage potential, there probably won't be a need for counseling. Relationships that are still in their early stages should not have major compounding issues yet, because there has not been enough time invested to warrant counseling, therefore pre-marriage coaching is likely the choice. However, if major issues and problems are detected at the start of a relationship it is probably related to one of two things. First, the issues arising are probably not a "we" issue but rather a "you" issue. These problems could be stemming from unresolved past hurts and pains being triggered from one or both partners. If this is the case, I recommend you get counseling separately to develop a plan of action to resolve the issues on your own before moving forward in the relationship too quickly. Doing this will help that person work through his or her issues of the past in a safe environment so he or she can be fully present moving forward in the relationship when the time is right. Remember you must bring 100 percent of yourself to the relationship to be successful.

The second thing your early issues could be attributed to is the fact that maybe you both are just so different that you are not compatible with one another. It is like trying to fit a square peg in a round hole. It just won't work. This should be a red flag for anyone who finds himself in a situation where these incompatibilities cause such major issues. When this is the case, seeking coaching from an objective standpoint could be very helpful in pointing you both in the right direction.

As you examine where you are in your relationship and identify your need for coaching, it might bring on some apprehension. This often stems from the fact that in many communities, going to talk to anyone outside the household and sharing personal business is considered taboo. So now, I want you to release the possible weight and fear that seeking independent advice can bring and view your marriage preparation as marriage education or training. Most working people, no matter the career, have had to take some type of class or training in preparation for the job or career they have, even if they have never stepped onto a college campus. There is nearly no career that you could embark on that would not require some type of training or education so my question is, "why do we not put the same investment into marriage"? If we are willing to train for a job which is only one aspect of our lives, we must put that same or greater effort into marriage! Marriage is not for the faint of heart and should not be taken lightly. No matter what you call it, with the proper training, education or coaching, you can maximize your potential to succeed in your marriage.

As I stated earlier, Bruce and I only had one pre-marriage counseling session before we got married which was totally inadequate. As a result, we ended up having to seek spiritual and professional counseling several years into our marriage to combat the issues we were having because we did not do the work up front. See, either way, you have to do the work. It's always better to seek wise counsel before there are issues. We have found counseling to be very helpful because it provided an objective voice. According to Drs. Les and Leslie Parrott, statistics show couples who succeed, gain the knowledge they need before they settle into destructive patterns that often lead to divorce. In fact, couples are 31% less likely to get divorced if they get some sort of pre-marriage training before they marry (Stanley et al., 2006). Not only that, couples who participate in pre-marriage programs experience a 30% increase in marital success and fulfillment over those who do not participate (Caroll & Doherty, 2003).

Team Aspect

One important aspect of any relationship is to understand that you are both on the same team. I like using the metaphor of teams when discussing relationships because everyone can relate. Whether you have played sports in school, been a part of intramurals, participated in a team as a class-work assignment or a team at work, we all generally understand the concept of teams. I have often heard the phrase, "there is no I in team" which is so true. I want you to think about how you show up in romantic relationships to determine what the word "team" looks like for you. I want you to know that the way you feel you show up in your relationship is most likely not how your mate sees you. I want you to put yourself in your significant other's place for a moment. Think back to conversations you have had, reactions, and experiences. Think through the decisions you made in various situations. How did you make others feel in those moments?

I also use the metaphor of teams because I think it helps us understand the level of harmony and compromise needed for the success of the relationship. When you think of teams, you must know that success lies heavily upon the players' ability to all play their respective positions in concert. Let's look at football for instance, there are various positions and all of them are needed for the team to win. Everyone can't be the quarterback, the running back, the linebacker or whichever position you deem as most important. Many times in relationships we like to take the position of star player or we go the stark opposite and don't participate at all and function as bench-warmers. The person on the bench is not going to help the team win because they are not in the game; neither will the star player that is showboating because he feels he can do it all on his own. When you think about the dynamics of a team think about all the needed elements that make that team great and figure out if you have those elements in the players on your team.

Pre-Marriage Coaching

So, what does pre-marriage coaching do? It helps you build your team. The main take-away of this book is the importance of getting you prepared and in the mindset of "we not me". If you want to be married, stay married and enjoy marriage you must not think of yourself as an individual any longer, but rather make unselfish decisions that will be best for the two of you. A team can't be successful if it has players only thinking of themselves. Pre-marriage coaching is going to help you condition and get stronger so that when unexpected plays come or you hit opposition, you will have the trust and respect built to overcome. Imagine in the sports world, being thrown together with someone to play in a game that you had not practiced with prior. It would be awkward, scary and quite intimidating. You wouldn't know what to anticipate from the other player. You wouldn't know their style, how they handle pressure, if they're a sore loser or better yet, if they are a team player. All of these things are imperative to find out before you enter the game of marriage. Marriage can be great, but only as rewarding as the time you invest into it. No team goes out expecting to score when they haven't put in the work. The same can be said in your relationship. Issues must be conveyed, addressed and resolved before saying "I do".

Now is the time to decide and I would love to help you. I provide pre-marriage coaching for dating, engaged and newly married couples. I help couples leverage their unique strengths and work through weaknesses for relationship success. With the right tools in hand, you will have everything you need to construct a solid foundation. If you are ready, so am I. Let's start the journey today! I am waiting for you!

THE OG

CHAPTER EIGHT NOTES:

CHAPTER EIGHT:

Reflection & Application

1. How are you showing up as a team player in your relationship? How do you define that in your relationship?

_____

_____

_____

_____

_____

_____

_____

_____

_____

_____

2. What are your goals for a pre-marriage coaching session?

_____

_____

_____

_____

_____

_____

_____

_____

References

1. Carroll, Jason S & Doherty, William G. "Evaluating the Effectiveness of Pre-Marriage Prevention Programs: A Meta-Analytic Review of Outcome Research". Family Relations, V. 52, 105-118. 2003

2. Collins, Gary R. Christian. *Coaching: Helping Others Turn Potential into Reality*: Second Edition, Colorado Springs, Colorado: Nav Press, 2009.

3. Parrott, L., & Parrott, L., (2020). *SYMBIS Facilitator Training Manual*. Seattle: Loveology

4. Stanley, Scott M., Amato, Paul., Johnson, Christine A., & Markman, Howard J. "Pre-Marital Education, Marital Quality and Marital Stability: Findings From A Large Random Household Survey". *Journal of Family Psychology*, V. 20, 117-126.

5. Stewart, John. *Bridges Not Walls: A Book About Interpersonal Communication*. 11th ed, Dubuque, India: McGraw-Hill., 2012.

6. Todeschi, Kevin J., *Edgar Cayce on Soul Mates: Unlocking the Dynamics of Soul Attraction*. Virginia Beach, Virginia: A.R.E. Press. 1999.

7. Wright, H. Norman. "Coaching Couples in Good Communication". Video Lecture. Liberty University Online. MLCM107: Lynchburg, Virginia. 2017

8. "Is It Best To Wait For A Soul Mate or Love The One You're With?" *Jet Magazine.*, V. 104(2):34. July 7, 2003. Retrieved from https://search-ebscohost-com.ezproxy.liberty.edu/login.aspx?direct=true&db=f5h&AN=10149223&site=ehost-live&scope=site.

ABOUT THE AUTHOR:
OLAUNDA G. GREEN

Olaunda G. Green, affectionately known as, "The OG", is the founder and CEO of *OG Coaching, LLC* in Raleigh, North Carolina. As an entrepreneur, public speaker, minister, life coach, relationship strategist, wife and mom, the OG is committed to helping you make the right call!

The OG provides pre-marriage coaching for dating, engaged and newly-married couples as well as pre-marital classes and small group sessions. Olaunda also facilitates and presents as a keynote speaker at faith-based organizations, conferences, trainings and seminars. The OG teaches winning strategies for relationship success by encouraging clients to think critically. Olaunda's wit and candor inspire audiences of various backgrounds through her ability to interlace experience with tutelage.

Olaunda holds a Bachelor of Science in Community Health Education from North Carolina Central University and a Master of Arts in Human Services Counseling with a Life Coaching Cognate from Liberty University. She is also a certified Saving Your Marriage Before It Starts (SYMBIS) Assessment Facilitator. Olaunda has been married to her loving husband for 15 years and they have a 9-year-old daughter.

getpublished@sheropublishing.com

S H E R O P U B L I S H I N G . C O M

Made in the USA
Columbia, SC
18 August 2020